HOORAY
FOR ME!

BY REMY CHARLIP & LILIAN MOORE
PAINTINGS BY VERA B. WILLIAMS
TRICYCLE PRESS ◉ BERKELEY, CALIFORNIA

HOORAY
FOR ME!

Tricycle Press
an imprint of Ten Speed Press
PO Box 7123
Berkeley, California 94707
www.tricyclepress.com

Library of Congress Cataloging-in-Publication Data
Charlip, Remy.
        Hooray for me! / by Remy Charlip & Lilian Moore, paintings by Vera B. Williams
                p. cm.
        Originally published: New York: Parents Magazine Press, 1975.
        Summary: Explores an individual's relationship to family, friends, and even pets.
        ISBN-13: 978-1-58246-201-1 pbk / 978-1-58246-201-1 hc
        ISBN-10: 1-58246-201-1 pbk / 1-883672-43-0 hc
        1. Family—Juvenile literature. 2. Children—Family relationships—Juvenile literature.
3. Self-perception—Juvenile literature. [1. Family. 2. Individuality.] I. Moore, Lilian.
II. Williams, Vera B., ill. III. Title.
HQ 744.C47 1996
306.85—dc20   96-2449   CIP   AC

First Tricycle Press printing, 1996
First paperback printing, 2007
Printed in Singapore

1 2 3 4 5 6 — 10 09 08 07

SON
DAUGHTER
BROTHER
FIRST COUSIN
SECOND COUSIN
THIRD COUSIN
NEPHEW
GREAT-GRANDFATHER
GREAT-UNCLE
STEPFATHER
FATHER
UNCLE
HALF-BROTHER

WIFE
FRIEND
BROTHER-IN-LAW
MOTHER
NIECE
GRANDSON
SISTER
GRANDMOTHER
HALF-SISTER
WHOSE SISTER?

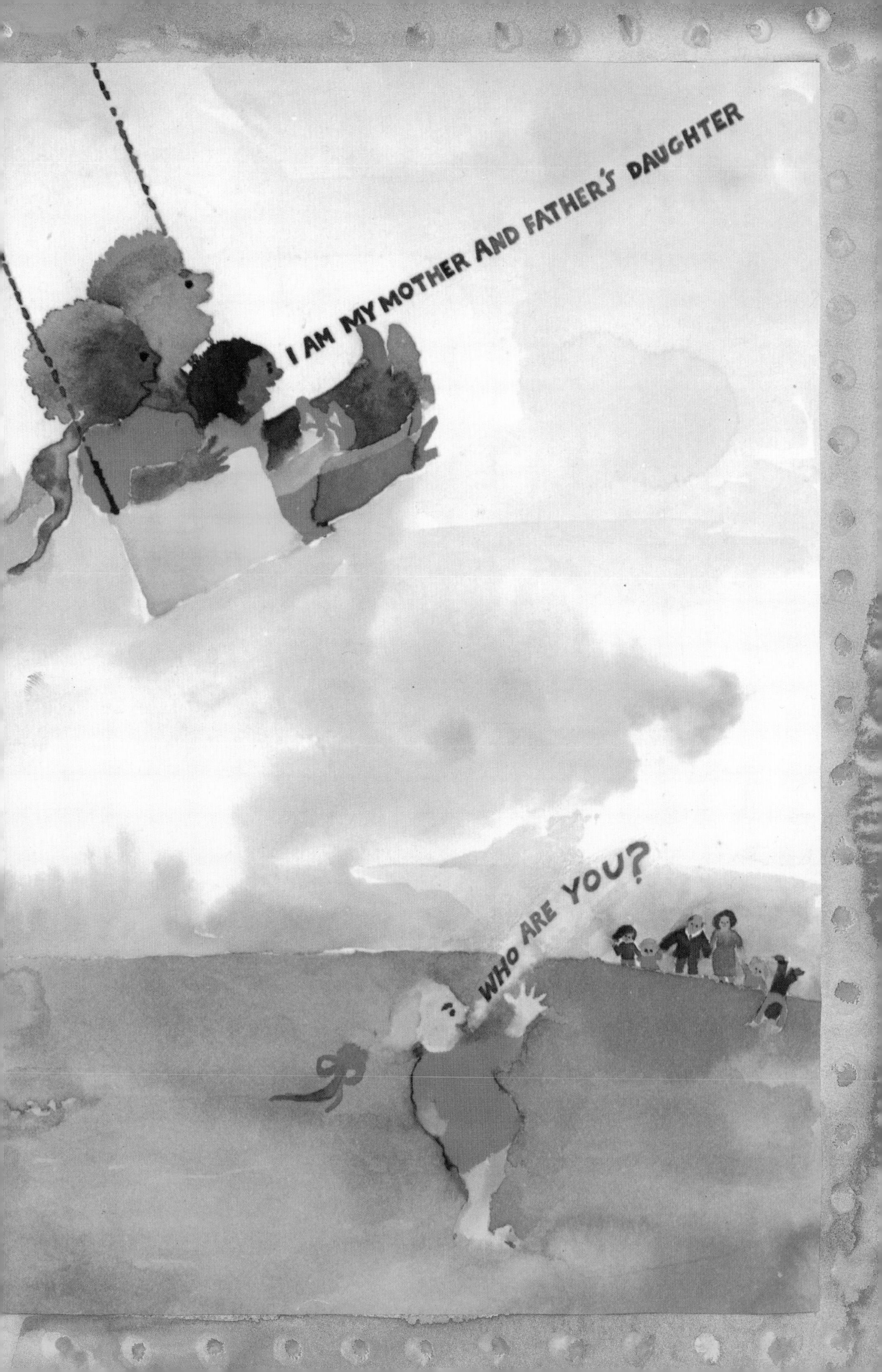
I AM MY MOTHER AND FATHER'S DAUGHTER
WHO ARE YOU?

I AM MY NIECE AND NEPHEW'S AUNT

I AM MY AUNT'S NEPHEW

I AM MY COUSIN'S COUSIN

I WOULD LIKE YOU TO MEET MY MOTHER
AND FATHER AND MY GRANDMOTHERS AND
GRANDFATHERS AND MY GREAT-GRANDMOTHERS
AND GREAT-GRANDFATHERS AND MY GREAT-
GREAT-GRANDMOTHERS AND GREAT-GREAT-
GRANDFATHERS AND MY GREAT-GREAT-GREAT-
GRANDMOTHERS AND GREAT-GREAT-GREAT-
GRANDFATHERS AND MY GREAT-GREAT-GREAT-
GREAT-GRANDMOTHERS AND GREAT-GREAT-
GREAT-GREAT-GRANDFATHERS WHICH MAKES
ME NOT ONLY A KITTEN BUT A GRANDKITTEN
AND A GREAT-GRANDKITTEN AND A GREAT-
GREAT-GRANDKITTEN AND A GREAT-GREAT-
GREAT-GRANDKITTEN AND A GREAT-GREAT-
GREAT-GREAT-GRANDKITTEN
ISN'T THAT GREAT?

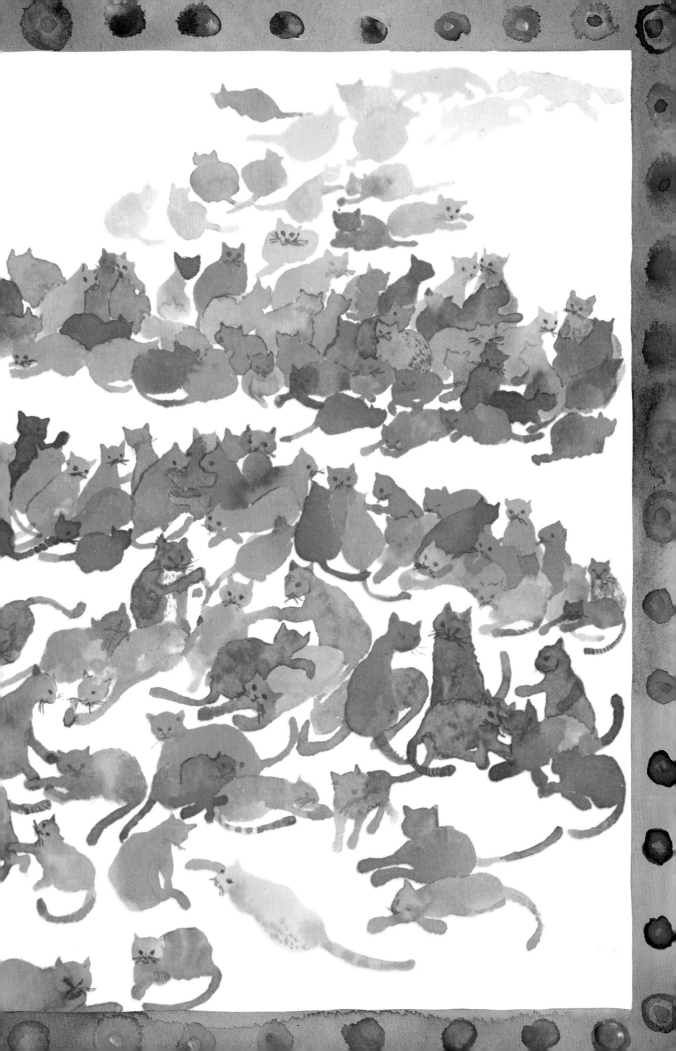

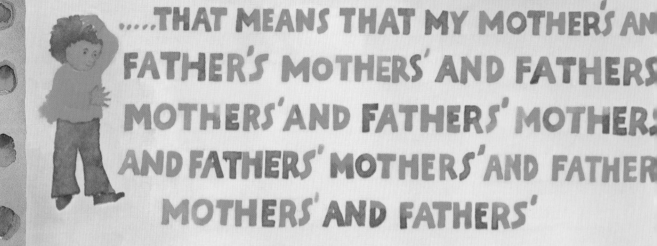

.....THAT MEANS THAT MY MOTHER'S AN
FATHER'S MOTHERS' AND FATHERS
MOTHERS' AND FATHERS' MOTHERS
AND FATHERS' MOTHERS' AND FATHER
MOTHERS' AND FATHERS'

GREAT

GREAT

GREAT

GREAT

GRAND

CHILD IS

?

..... CAN YOU GUESS?

ME

AND ME

ME TOO

ME TOO

AND ME

ME TOO

AND ME AND THAT'S NOT ALL I AM.....

I'M MY DREAM'S DREAMER

I'M A STAR

I AM MY BEST FRIEND'S BEST FRIEND

(SOMETIMES)

I'M A FEEDER

I'M AN EATER

I'M MY FAMILY'S DISHWASHER

I'M THIS BOOK'S READER (HOORAY FOR ME!)

WHATEVER I WAS
WHATEVER I'LL BE
HOORAY FOR YOU!
HOORAY FOR ME!

WHATEVER YOU DO
WHATEVER YOU'LL BE
HOORAY FOR YOU!
HOORAY FOR ME!

HOORAY FOR US!
WHATEVER WE BE
HOORAY FOR YOU!
HOORAY FOR ME!

HOORAY FOR ME!

HOORAY FOR YOU! AND ME! AND YOU!

HOORAY FOR ME

HOORAY FOR YOU! AND ME!

HOORAY FOR ME

HOORAY FOR YOU!

HOORAY FOR ME!

AND YOU!

HOORAY FOR YOU!

HOORAY FOR TWO!

HOORAY FOR THREE!!

HOORAY FOR ME!

HOORAY FOR YOU!

HOORAY FOR WHO?

OORAY FOR YOU! HOORAY FOR WE!
HOORAY FOR ME!
RAY FOR YOU!
ME!
WE!
HE!
SHE!
HOORAY FOR ME!
OORAY FOR ME! HOORAY FOR YOU!
HOORAY FOR GOO!